NOW IN COLOR

NOW IN COLOR

Jacqueline Balderrama

perugia
PRESS

FLORENCE, MASSACHUSETTS
2020

Perugia Press extends deeply felt thanks to the many individuals whose generosity made the publication of *Now in Color* possible. Perugia Press is a tax-exempt, nonprofit 501(c)(3) corporation publishing first and second books of poetry by women. To make a tax-deductible donation, please contact us directly or visit our website.

Book design by Jacqueline Balderrama, Rebecca Olander, and Jeff Potter

Cover photograph used with permission of Enrique Balderrama

Author photograph by Jesus Huerta Jr.

Library of Congress Cataloging-in-Publication Data

Names: Balderrama, Jacqueline, 1990- author.
Title: Now in color / Jacqueline Balderrama.
Description: Florence, Massachusetts : Perugia Press, 2020.
Identifiers: LCCN 2020030309 | ISBN 9780997807646 (paperback)
Subjects: LCSH: Mexican Americans--Poetry. | LCGFT: Poetry.
Classification: LCC PS3602.A59525 N69 2020 | DDC 811/.6--dc23
LC record available at https://lccn.loc.gov/2020030309

Perugia Press
PO Box 60364
Florence, MA 01062
editor@perugiapress.org
perugiapress.org

for my family

CONTENTS

esperanza *[ES-pear-AHN-sah]* noun (f) :

Migration is written on this green heartache
of home, once its own discovery of water—
the Aztecs' Metztlixcictlico, meaning
place in the center of the moon.

Some are used to hopes being where they've been.
But singing one octave is Kansas to Oz. For a while,

my father didn't know that the movie changed
to Technicolor since the family TV was black and white.

NOW IN COLOR

Migratory patterns of monarchs continue
        alongside gray wolves, armadillos, coyotes.

Now *paper,* now *papel*—we learn to listen in different ways,
        and again, someone asks for the source of me
                as if water could stop or would.

Agents dress us in the terms of their casting calls—
        anonymous beneath the sombrero, or fiery Latina, or gardener,
                or alien, or drug lord.

Now Maria Montez, Katy Jurado, Rita Hayworth watch themselves
        in the funny mirror.

And my mother shakes her head for the childhood dog
        the neighbors took in, then abandoned in the desert.

Now the wildfires on the San Bernardino Mountains—
        at night, families set out lawn chairs to watch the flames.

And a man electrifies his fences and shows the reporter large photos
        of bodies he's found beneath his trees.

Now the radio is breathless...

The television like an escape portal streams color
        through undraped windows.

But inside we are still here

fumbling to turn on the light or floating down in our chairs,
        wishing the room to unleash its plum, its marigold, the blue
                of our jeans, the white walls covered with frames.

We peel heavy shadows from broomsticks, coils of rope, strangers,
                    admitting, somehow, we can still have good days.

Somewhere desert poppies will grow—with all of this
                                        —and without it—

MOJAVE DESERT

During high noon, you enter the stars until you're blinded,
then share the clouded waters of arthropods.
Who would believe they too had eyes

before they were pressed like stamps in the strata
rising within the mountain, and you with them
pulled into color and fanned.

Some want to know how choppers can touch
down on the desert floor without sound
or disturbance when always there are clouds of dust.

Here, shells remain from Patton's army maneuvers
preparing for North Africa in 1930.
Call this place *rain shadow*.

You draw in the missing
pieces of trilobite on a pad of paper,
place the fossil fragment on top like a weight.

MEXICO AS MEXICO, 1914

Mexican soldiers of the Revolución play their shades
through Hollywood cameras—gray, charcoal, ash, slate—

for *The Life of General Villa,* except the bullets are real
and there's nothing special about effects.

Battles set during daylight mean you can see
when a man falls, the orchestra moves on without him.

In one recovered reel, a rag threads through
the shrapnel hole in someone's leg.

In others, the backstory filmed in California
where a young Villa rears a trick horse

spinning the way it will in *Birth of a Nation.*
The rest melts to silver drops.

But you're asking for one quarter of my blood,
and for a footfall on the southern border—

before my father was born and my grandfather too,
before his father worked in the shipyards and in the orchards—

and for someone who looks like me but isn't.
You must rewind to this place to know

it was post *The Outlaw's Revenge,*
post the raid on Columbus, New Mexico, 1916

when the original footage was recast
as hero-turned-bandit.

And somewhere between here and Satevó,
my ancestors escape the way steam rises from fire.

oscuro *[ohs-COO-ro]* adjective :

And color is the first reason
it seems I must learn Spanish.

Much is left in dark waters.
Light warps into quivering patterns.

Different kinds of desire shape under this red umbrella,
beneath these slender trees.

LA LLAMADA

—after the painting by Remedios Varo

No one uses the word *call* anymore to say, *I came to your door.*
When I heard your voice, I was lined against the wall
with all the others, or we were being separated
from the wall, the lines covering our hats and clothes
—a thick apron of bark. Such is the difficulty of attachment.
Had we become an absence? Our faces expressionless, our eyes
closed as if we were part of some dream. But you were the one
in orange tethered to a star, flame-like and magnetic.
This, we saw without opening our eyes.

Listen . . .

A man sings about the devil to the kick-drum beat of his washer.

Women on a flight home talk about having and not having children.

Anonymous lions roar when a button's pushed at the zoo's big-cat exhibit.

The sound waves become heat, become energy,
        which is the only account I can give for your glowing.

STUDY OF TWO HANDS

We hold fruits deciding how good they are
avocados / Saturn peaches / cherries / plums

        Our shapes
        we've memorized another way
        balancing and passing through doors

        so that running the brush on paper
        might always do our will

We will turn the self-portrait / face the mirror
where our reflections will look in on each other
the way peach halves regard their center

        But the mirror's portrait doesn't
        match my reflection
        Wide-eyed and misshapen / it may have

        achieved all that strangers expected
        of me / Or it may only know

the meaning / of the light and the dark
laid side by side on the palette before mixing

        Nevertheless it is me too / in the mirror
        beside the portrait

        I hold it like a sign / which reads
        My skin has only been where I have been

FRAGMENTED APOLOGY, 2006

—after California Senate Bill 670, enacting the "Apology Act
for the 1930s Mexican Repatriation Program"

When the knocking comes / county agents are on the porch
telling "Mexicans" / *You should go in two weeks*
Here are the tickets / Here's your destination

In raids / hundreds at La Placita Park / detained
for papers / vans idling in the peripheries
while their children at school / wait

And threats / for some families / are real enough
to leave / How can this be called / *voluntary*
As a heartbreak / As a life packed and thrown across the hills

Who knew and said nothing / and still
says nothing / Who went turning off the house lights
because no one was / home

Imagine the people in the train car / the girl whispering
the moon is following her
to the make-believe town / become real / become

vacant looks on her parents' eyes / In reflection
a little oasis of nothing / and you / lucky to know
someone / or not / Some can speak the language

or can't / One woman must paint her belonging
until there's a bridge / and in the distance
a steeple

relato *[ray-LAH-toe]* noun (f) :

Fragments underwater and distant
gleam like starfish
sure to dry into brittle, pale selves.

I've learned to collect what's scattered,
learned to set them here

on the chance odd ends whisper.

TO REACH THE MIDDLE OF THE OCEAN

When Pearl Harbor is bombed, my grandfather's in California
watching *Swamp Water*—gray trees, hanging moss,
recorded chirps and buzzes from frogs, insects, birds.
A father fights for his son to not disappear, and still the young
Dana Andrews dirties his face as he searches for his hound
in the deep unknown. My grandfather thinks of alligators
below the rim of black water, of fluffy ducks above,
then slender deer. Jungle this close to home is unbelievable.
More likely, Anne Baxter, barefoot and ragged and biting,
will somehow fall in love when—
                              darkness.

All Service Men Report
projected in her place.

SANTA CATALINA

When the wealthy flee Catalina, you move in
along with antiaircraft guns, observation towers.
Still, the buffalo, brought for a movie they were never in,
go on living their lives. No one's worried
that after so many reinventions, the island might
finally roll over and swim away. Feral cats roam its city,
feral goats the sunny brush. From excavation, remnants
of fishers and traders signal they too paddled to its shores.
Now, you learn to unload cargo in the harbor.
Others knot trousers for use as flotation,
and maybe this will save them from the deep curtain of kelp,
its flickers of light and gaping chasm. I learn
some hotel rooms were converted to barracks.
But you say you were in a wooden hut with three others
and never swam through enflamed water.
In that hut, sunk in the shadows of early winter,
the four of you listen to murmurs and light footsteps
on damp leaves. One fellow asks, *What are you?*
He means why are you brown.
He says, *Aren't you ashamed of it?*

USS *RANDOLPH* DAMAGED, 1945

Decades after glimpsing the suicide dive
from your nearby merchant ship, you read
how twenty-four Frances bombers left Formosa.
Due to poor navigation, only two arrived.
For a moment, you imagine twenty-two pilots
descending through the darkening net
of water shadows until colors go as far as they can.
Two planes against five hundred ships.
In the reverse image—you might never have known,
might never have been. You remember
how easy it was to "slip" overboard.
At a union meeting, one fellow said, *If I disappear,*
I want to let you know who is after me.

What was left of the story shuttered along the coast
without notice for forty years. You watched
your children grow, their families too.
When veteran benefits arrive in 1988
you say, *Too late for any more school.*
And your ship—found in the names of vacation rentals
on a Florida peninsula—the *Cape San Blas,*
now likely metal repurposed in the sides of other ships.

salvaje *[sahl-VAH-heh]* adjective :

In grief, we cannot explain the body's
tenderness, its heaviness.

Without tears, the dog nurses
an old shoe for weeks.

RESONANT FREQUENCY

On the afternoon the bulldozers came
for the trees in the field past her backyard,
my sister imagined she'd take in the two horses,
who on all other days would be sleeping in the shade,
standing in the buzzing grasses, and later
eating apples from my sister's hands
once she climbed through
the loose slats of the fence.

In her house, the horses are civil,
stepping on newspaper, admiring her upright piano,
but neither she nor the horses can bear the groans
of cottonwood and sweetgum taking their falls
the way swans land on water—waving branches,
a splash of dust and leaves, their wings now
folded and still.

It's this groaning, she says, *from the trees
and from other things.* I hear it too
from the news on washed-up refugees, children
at the border, the unspeakable crouched
so flat, at times we forget what madness is.

WATER, 2014

Their homes have melted in the crossfire.
Children bring water, as much as they can carry

from Honduras, El Salvador, Guatemala, Mexico.
That same week over a thousand children have crossed,

coyotes pointing them toward border patrol, then disappearing
the way they came. It might mean relatives, court dates,

or untreated colds, cement floors on which to sleep. At night,
relics of the desert are socks, medicine boxes,

tires dragged over one's footprints. A prayer hinges on the wings
of a gilded flicker foraging the ground for ants.

In migrations, which ended here—an interview of checked pockets.
Discovered bones are held at the morgue for questioning.

They *had* found the blue-capped water by a creosote bush—
promised colored caps of full gallons, azul for water, rojo for juice—

sticking up from beneath the desert floor.
But someone had uprooted them and stabbed the plastic.

ZERO, 2018

Keep saying what you saw, and before you are sore
I will sing, and before I am parched, another.
Sing *cero, cero, cero.*

The round of our voices might roll back
our thoughts, might recollect the scattered photos,
the children's cries, that hot summer within
the border's belly—
        cages
                    no clocks
                              barely shadows
to tell the time

and the backs of people on long, narrow benches,

the way it grew crowded

                  and transformed from cement floors

and crinkled, silver blankets

                  into many, distant rooms.

Cero for the mourning O of outrage, for the empty shell
drawn first to signify an accounted nothingness,
for the meaningless words and hurried signatures
on bright white pages.

sonar *[soh-NAHR]* verb :

On the phone was the ghost again—
Hello? Hello?

My grandfather retells the time
he *blew it* leaving high school.

AFTERLIFE

In the cemetery we find names, symbols for different faiths.
We imagine the body at rest, as we're told.
We imagine other traditions like other shoes.

For Mexico City, painted petals fill eye sockets, nose cavities, mouths.
Once a year, purchased marigolds guide spirits
to altars, to picnics beside graves.

For Rome, martyrs from catacombs display wealth in the afterlife:
motionless—ruby, seed pearl, and emerald cover the bones
now in church. Now what matters.

For Cairo, the mummy will reinhabit its rooms
storing furniture, cups, clothes. The body
a vessel to be filled.

Imagine the Andes too—the mountain which asked for nothing
where small bodies curled in ice last for centuries
undiscovered. Now found.

We touch our skin, looking through to the veins
as if this ink could speak our end. Rivers find theirs,
spilling one into the next into the next.

What of our plan? We don't say it in words.
But my love and I think we will decompose into one another
—this will be my hand and his.

THE DEAD DREAM US

1.

Ghosts pass between homes, between cuts of earth,
between hills and rivers—impressions
rippling the gown of a giantess.

Those-who-look-for-her climb into her pressed palms.
They inhale roses, listen to stars chime like church bells.
From there, all the world could fit in her hand.

2.

For the dead, we want to grieve,
for you and your labor, for the churches built
from the stones of your cities.

In the same breath, we must admit, a people grew
despite and from this suffering—its hopeful crossings,
its schools of erasure, its white and brown parents.
And I am a person from this origin
who did not suffer as much.

3.

Some say Our Lady of Guadalupe is an assimilation.
Then she is also mine and my family's too.
It is difficult to admit this without judgment,
or without wondering if I am a kind of dream
or disappointment for the dead who came before.

The last time my grandfather visits his brother
in Mexico, he says he's watched all his grandchildren
go to college. And wasn't this what he hoped?

But in town with his brother's friends,
he is so old, he can't remember the language.
Embarrassed, he can only nod, his lips pressed in.

ULITHI

You enjoyed being nowhere,
how men were equally small against the merchant ships,
small against the Western Pacific.

Front lines, you thought, dissolved like salt,
salt water to rinse a sore throat.

Back and forth, mariners moved with the cargo,
though some Navy called you *riffraff, draft dodgers*.

Picture gray masses anchored beneath sun:
battle wagons, your cargo vessel.
It was beach day.

You'd finished wiping your rag over table rims.
Ulithi suffered paradise—the islands, the guns.

Over the phone, *Ulithi* sounded like *Ulysses*
marred by the water, the fish like shrapnel confetti.

Below, an oil tanker sunk in the shallows,
cracked, twisted—a stunned giant.

From satellite mapping, Ulithi's lagoon and islands
dotting the rim of an undersea volcano
are invisible,

such that, you might still be drinking
those two warm beers, might still be
eighteen, looking down through clear water.

rueda *[roo-EH-da]* noun (f) :

To make pinwheels and paper rosettes, I'm told
to begin with squares and rectangles, folding

edges into the center. They spin as if they've forgotten
this origin of steps. We too forget our feet.

STUDY OF SELF-PORTRAIT

I hate / that / I love transformation montages

> The arctic fox sheds its brown fur for the winter promise
> Testing the snow it dives / again and again to color beneath

Here is *Before* / Here, fast-forwarding to the smile

> The actress fills in her brows / She is the artist and the canvas
> enough to select a new name

We hope we're all as pretty underneath / all American sweethearts

> And then do most stop asking / *Where where where*
> / soft sirens / *are you from*

Rita Hayworth never televises her first true makeover

> Neither does she pick her name like a fruit
> She revises it to her mother's / adding a *y*
> for sounds / always intended

Rewind to Margarita Carmen Cansino

> Imagine editing yourself / Reconcile
> that after a hit / they'll still place you in B movies
> that after marrying a prince / you'll still be lonely in crowds

Or rewind to The Queen of Technicolor's / María África Gracia Vidal

> Remain / Become / Remain / Become / Remain / Become

THE QUEEN OF TECHNICOLOR, 1943

My grandmother is fifteen, entranced by color.
Islanders paddle to shore with loads of papaya,
the ocean sweeping the sand, spilling from the screen.

All eyes ahead. It's Maria Montez,
this time royalty in plumeria headdress.
Yellow, coral, violet bloom around her and in her.

My grandmother's family changes the spelling of their last name
to match: Móntes to Montez. Mountains to mountains.
Part of the giantess exists in her.

And it's true. It's *Celia Montez, like the movie star.*
Montez, The Queen of Technicolor, is always in love,
or in the moment right before being in love.

With a stern face, my grandmother's mamá tells her,
The Queen is not serving her husband enchiladas and beans.
She is not telling her children to pray. My grandmother doesn't care.

Montez's sleepy eyes call the audience in. And this is her
secret: If you were like her—a princess in the tropics, a Persian queen,
Cobra Woman—you'd be in love, too, or about to be.

For my grandmother, the hum of her Spanish accent
under the English words is the fisherman's line in the meet cute.
She, like Montez, is home in a paradise, from which all colors illumine,

sent forth on waves to the shore, to the promenade, to the dance hall
where girls like her wait for their stories to end in a kiss.
She will know what happens soon enough, when

at nineteen, my grandmother will marry Enrique,
her last name disappearing in those starry children
chasing one another through their Anaheim motel.

She will outlive Montez, who dies in her reducing bath at thirty-nine,
and she will say her father's name to herself, *Pedro Móntes,*
will recall his singing "De Colores" on the local radio.

MY RITA HAYWORTH

My Rita first poses
in a white two-piece by the pool.
Black to Auburn to Strawberry Blond
to Red to Platinum, her hairline
seared by electric currents.
My Rita as Covergirl, as Salome, as Gilda
plastered on the atomic bomb
for its first testing
in the Western Pacific.
The papers say she is
its *christening*.
They mean *sex-bomb*.
Perfect for the mystery
of what will happen.

Margarita Carmen Cansino
is mistaken for a stranger.
But my Rita is *the real thing*.
We drop her from the clouds
over white sand atolls.
We watch her fall
in and out of love,
fall in and out of marriage,
fall until there are stars
around her head.

We say this is part of her
dance routine. *Get up! Get up!*
And when she does,
she'll fling back her hair,
forgetting she's always
fragmented, always

in at least two places at once.
But what did she tell her daughters
about love? Beauty?
Will the cue cards gently
map the lines when the memory
of them is gone, and Rita too?
We might act like we know,
might dub out her singing
for our own.

ALTERNATE WAYS TO PAINT

—glancing off Pablo Picasso's
paintings and drawings, 1890–1955

1. The Picador

On your birthdays you added a polka-dot bow tie, an old hat.
You sang Soupy Sales. The party is watching you:
a woman in a white shawl, the man with the flat nose
whose name you may never know. You feel
you've been sitting in the sun too long.

2. Public Garden

Your father told his parents that your mother washed clothes
even though it wasn't true. It wasn't true
that she was three years older either.
To everyone else, she looked like Jackie Kennedy—
though she'd never admit to the imitation.
Her face finds its way back in your third daughter.
Now it's all blurred. It's warm colors, like trees
in a hot wind before a storm,
like women in aprons going home.

3. The Two Saltimbanques:
Harlequin and His Companion

Your first date is a double. She wears a Spanish dress,
a pink belt. You both have borscht with 7&7s.
It's a big table. You find yourself in the corner with her,
while across the booth, her brother and your cousin
are already married. She's cute. Your hands now curled
about your chin, shaped to interlink.

4. Life

came slippery and cold—first snow, first snowball to the groin.
Lying flat on your back, you're traced with chalk. You still carry that
cutout. Consoled, fetal, you wonder what swallowed you.
This woman is your wife, you, her husband
looking back on yourself, thinking time a circle.
You regret those dips into blue.

5. The Actor

Your wife catches you playing Hamlet in the bathroom.
You're at the mirror crying. She pulls off your funny clothes,
takes you to bed. Once more, you're pieces
of blue and yellow, neither wanting to touch.

6. Family of Jugglers

You remember studying law. You remember cleaning
motel rooms in the summer. That memory, a Polaroid photo.
On Sundays you attend church with your wife, your children.
Work is a circus of criminals and manila folders. You're finding
it easier to believe people can murder. Bar chairs. Billiard balls.

7. Harlequin on Horseback

You learned to drive late afternoon somewhere in Anaheim.
Your father stumbled into the passenger seat. He put it in gear
and pointed. You put on his hat and shoes. You drove
through the night, through taillights reddening the rain.

8. Still Life with Lemons

The cantaloupe tastes like candy, your wife says,
but you don't taste it when the day has been pounding.
It could have been an illusion, all of it, the whole day.
What color is cantaloupe anyway?

9. Harlequin Leaning

In your study, you sleep for a while. You wear your father's
maritime hat and a little smile. Outside one daughter is on the phone
walking in circles. The parakeets are ringing their bells.
You think about quitting again.

10. The Chess

Sometimes you think you'd rather be hit in the face.
You don't like attending socials. It's an infinity of martini
glasses. You think you see
a river or a horse this afternoon, in the faces
and circles and diamonds. Someone once told you
a horse in one's dreams means *desire*.
You think you have some kind of control.

11. Apple

Tart Granny Smith goading you on with that bright, yes green.
You found it on the floor, dusted in shadow.
You put it in your pocket for later.

12. The Dream

Your wife asks you to take her to Macy's.
She wants to pick out a pearl necklace.
At night when everyone's in bed,
you talk about moving to the country.
Though you dislike the outdoors, you know
you can see the stars there. You don't need
to say anything to anyone there.

13. Faun, Horse, and Bird

This time, in the mirror, you've changed. Smudges,
tears, a green shadow. You try to clean off the mirror,
and *it* tries to wipe away *you*.
You stand up. You climb into the nearest building.
You go shopping in antique stores for whatever you've forgotten.

14. Minotaur with Dead Horse in Front of a Cave Facing a Girl in Veil

It's the last time you put on this costume. The last time
you take your childhood back in your arms and try to make it move.
You wind it up. You push play. Nothing happens.
You leave the store, blocking your eyes from the brightness.

15. The Remains of Minotaur in a Harlequin Costume

You begin taking dance lessons and marriage counseling.
To the therapist, you say your wife doesn't understand.
You talk about your animal history—
you talk about the pets you've had, your whole life.

16. Boat of Naiads and Wounded Faun

After finding the bottle in the bathroom cabinet,
your wife confronts you. You are upset.
You must have horns, must be buried in the ocean
trying to dig your way through to the other side.
But the water is shallow, the bottom a scratched slate.
She and your daughters pull you out by the tail.

17. Untitled

Your portrait of Thomas More makes him look ambivalent.
You wonder what to do when one daughter stops
going to church, when another is all over the place,
when the youngest corrects your golf swing
you'd learned from books and TV.

18. Cat Eating a Bird

The pets sometimes show you where they're from,
how they could survive without you. How economical
they are. Daughters ask you to pick up the body halves of gophers,
the feathers clumped on the ground. Only the cat is quite proud.
You carry the corpse in a wrapping of plastic to the trash.
It won't be picked up until Tuesday.

19. Night Fishing at Antibes

You're old. Your daughters eat ice cream and watch you.
From their bicycles, the scene is collage:
fluttering triangles, spiraling lights, you kneeling.
Never having caught a fish, you're returning to the origin,
a man in the garden, your companion taking a drink.

20. Don Quixote

You first learned to draw birds as *m*'s in kindergarten.
Now, you lean in to hear the humming,
to see if any are suspended against the white sky.
In its coarse simplicity, you recognize the sun,
that old horse.

cenote *[seh-NOH-teh]* noun (m) :

Tell me about underground lakes in Mexico.
The ground sighs into caves, and you're there.

I kiss my lover's ear, breathe gently into its small darkness.
From the grassy edge, we consider the rain.

A FIRE TO COOK

This afternoon in a Riverside taqueria,
my date orders us mango juice and tacos.
We squeeze lime over the food,
watch families wait with a basket of chips,
the kids closer to perfection than we may ever be.
A mound of masa sits by the flat stovetop.

He tells me where he visits family
there are courtyards with surrounding rooms,
explains the kitchen must have a fire to cook,
and when you shower, you pour water over your head
with a dipper from a bucket.
There, you inhale the bitter and salty stems of tomatoes,
the rising sting of de árbol chiles.
And when you do: you are the courtyard—
its succulents, dahlias, palo verde trees,
nopal cactus, its prickly pears, bougainvillea,
and glass shards embedded atop the walls
to keep the chickens in.

FINGER PUPPET IN THE LIKENESS OF FRIDA KAHLO

From the pedestal of a hand, she nods. Three flowers in her hair, red rebozo across her shoulders, Frida as a finger puppet speaks to children about beauty. Do they already know what is different about Frida's appearance? She faces the world through the stare in each wounded portrait—a deer saying, *pain comes in every color*; two Fridas in a wash of storm clouds; a woman rooted in recline. The window of her chest delivers a vine, and it's reaching toward you.

YOU AND I SAW ANIMALS

1.

Lion summertime swallowed us up year after year.
We sisters picked neighbors' apricots, peaches, nectarines.
We swung our legs—acrobats on ponies—from pedals to handlebars.

We puffed air into the nylon of our swimsuits
to make breasts like mermaids, the water holding them up.
That was when we started wearing swimsuits.

We were wetting our hair in front of our faces,
then rolling the damp sheets of it back
to look like George Washingtons,

the hose twirling in the pool
until the last warm day had already passed,
the water too cold to venture in.

2.

We listened to longer books on our parents' bed,
illustrated Greek mythology. How silly all those gods and grown-ups—
chasing the sun, opening boxes, looking back.

Odysseus had built that olive tree bed, each bedpost
a growing tree trunk. But Penelope was alone, sleeping
on the left or right side, then spread out in the middle.

Each night, it was as if we could undo our own weaving. We could
start the next day as the last, living it over, perfecting it.
It was as easy as unlacing our fingers from one another.

While Odysseus was off on one of his promises, we were sure
the bed had grown, lifted off the roof.
Inside became outside. Animals wandered closer, following light.

3.

We thought of lion summertime, speckled deer, antsy rabbits,
baboons, green parrots, and crows sidestepping her bed's branches,
invisible to the suitors, who, to their credit, only saw Penelope.

But the crows weren't there for love, just olives, which they took
in the mornings as they did on our street, when the fruit fell purple and fat.
Stepping on split olives on bedcovers, they made crow's-feet all over.

This was the story you told me in the attic of our garage.
I could feel the spotted fur of the leopard, the feathered necks
of flamingoes. We were all of those animals at once,

until you were bored waiting for love.
You flew down the attic's drop ladder, leaving me
in the rafters. You began to sing.

arroyo *[ah-RROY-oh]* noun (m) :

Most rivers I've grown with were shallow—
you could walk across them.

In the gutter, we sisters watched our leaf boats
float on carwash suds, disappear in drains.

Finding him at a bar, during the birth of his first child,
my great-uncle told my grandfather,
who told my father, *Nobody owes you a good time.*

IN BED WITH THE LION

—after photographs by Michael Rougier of Melanie Griffith and a lion
at her California home

They sleep, each covered by the red blanket. Lion's tail
plumes out from under like the thick cord of a church bell.

Or
they are awake, watching each other be still.
They compare hair and nails against the rosebud print of the sheets.

Or
they are pretending to sleep—one hiding from her mother,
one from its nature, which has never left. They lie quiet, as if dead.

Or
one is awake, watching the other sleep, considering the live-in trainer's
request that Mother, Daughter, and Lion use their *inside voices*.

Or
they are waiting for the photographer, waiting for the pool
where she can pull Lion's paws through her wet hair like a heavy brush.

Or
since the lion is apparently named Neil, they like to believe
in a world that would allow such things.

LION LIGHTS

We may never know what it's like for a predator to enter our gate
and drag away the cow / We may never know / what it is like to be
the predator found in the grass / then dragged into town
by the hind paws hearing *This is my territory* / *That is yours*

Cows didn't always live by the savanna / Neither did the boy
who leads them to grasslands / who says / *A lion for a cow*
What does it matter / after both lie still in the yard / the lions
still coming / The boy builds the compromise

in a modified car battery / linked to lights running off solar
after so many shunned scarecrows / hung
dewy and limp / At night / torch bulbs flash for the lions
glinting off their eyes / glinting off the dull cows' eyes

So the lions move toward zebra foals / The boy enters
in the morning with feed and draws the milk / We want to say
to ourselves *Lion is a thief* / *is a drunk driving their car*
into our tree / *is a mortician* / *who steals corneas* / But no

The lion / is a lion / was / will be a lion / We don't know
what a lion is outside / the cage / the channel / the big-cat rescue farm
How are we / outside the lion / Sometimes we're just straw
stuffed in old clothes / Sometimes we move / The lions move too

WITNESS

Even now, bodies are still found in the desert.

       I try to listen.

       Or am I *still* enough to return to dry grass in a landscape?
       As a child, I'd follow the cracks in the road like a treasure map.

Already, we have heard so much.

       A five-year-old read her letter to the pope:
       All immigrants just like my dad help feed this country.
       And scientists counted more microplastics in the ocean
       than stars in the Milky Way.

       My great-grandmother watched too many telenovelas,
       said, *Love him. Love him. Love him. Or leave him, now.*

Conviction is what we need

       in planting jugs of water in the desert border,
       in extending our hands—I heard
       we've sent something into deep space.

       Some write to preserve themselves,
       and others build churches the size of breadboxes
       to mark the sites of car crashes
       so we're sure to slow down.

criatura *[cree-ah-TOO-rah]* noun (f) :

In the animal, we look for our likenesses.
We think we see two people in the horse:

One steers with the front legs and head,
one, the back and tail, lifts the other to jump.

MIMICRY AT THE EXPENSE OF
MONTGOMERY CLIFT

They might be flies pretending to be bees,
but no one at the table can tell for sure
when they're constantly swerving,

and we're tired of distraction
even if BeeSpotter has the statement,
No mimic is perfect. This is not

slow motion. We're living at regular,
and therefore can't count
the number of wings.

> Flies: two / Bees: four
> Notice an elbowed antenna,
> slender or pollen-basket legs.

We only notice stripes.

> Bee Fly   Hover Fly   Robber Fly

> and it's getting dark...

Later, on television, Montgomery Clift
in *I Confess.* Here, too, is a fly dressed like a bee
—or a bee dressed like a fly—
a murderer in a priest's cassock
framing our hero.
What won't we do for preservation?

In three years, Clift will be

       in a car crash in the midst of another film,
       in surgeries to mimic a *before,* his face
       in that film hovering over his earlier look,
       flickering.

Everyone buys tickets to see the left side of his face
standing still, nearly emotionless.

Watching, my father keeps saying, *Before, after, before...*
How many times do we leave
a self and never return, thinking
there is relief, a garden, and dinner waiting?

SOME HORSES

Mustangs stand in corrals across from the prison grounds.
Some sleep. Some wander toward water
in the mouths of overturned tires.
Nearby, sweet-smelling blocks of hay dry in gated fields
while blackbirds scratch loose straw near the roadside.
The inmates learn to approach and gentle the horses.
It begins with running the hands along the shoulder,
walking beside one another.
The man notices what the horse may notice,
the sun at their backs, their overlapping shadows.

ACCOUNTABILITY FOR BLIND SHEEP

God is suspect when Chilean sheep go blind. *The NY Times* reports
it's ozone or pink eye, soon other reasons not to pray.

From the restaurant patio with my glass of ice water, I see a man
walk by—crumpled clothes, full beard, bucket hat. I see a woman,
pant leg tied over one knee, practice in the heat with her walker.

On my way home, I repeat: *blind sheep, homeless man, amputee*—
names, which are not names, strung through like beads.

I consider

> the man's parents
> the tired yellow buttons at the Natural History Museum
> the endings of Perry Mason, how neat
> Our Lady of Guadalupe statues.

Come morning, the statue in the side yard bows in prayer
while balancing on that little crescent, on that tiny angel.
She'll paint self-portraits with roses for Juan Diego
and the remembered, while I hear myself saying,
No thank you, not interested.

huerta *[WEAR-tah]* noun (f) :

I could live in this garden.

With fruit trees, with vegetables,
this is a working land.

Think of soup—as a child pulling leaves, berries, grass,
stirring a pail for dinner.

SPANISH LANGUAGE FILM HOUSE, 1930S

On Sundays, my grandfather's pop drives mamá, him, and his siblings
to his uncle's store for penny candy
and then to The California Theater on Main Street.

They follow the girl and her flashlight to their seats.
In his, my grandfather is just tall enough that the tips of his toes
may tap the floor when Carlos Gardel begins to sing.

Guitar in hand, his eyes squint, his head wavering as if he can envision
a kind fate, as if he can see my grandfather chewing candy
along with all the Spanish speakers who've come to hear him.

He sings to my grandfather's parents:
Sueño con el pasado que añoro,
el tiempo viejo que lloro y que nunca volverá.

And they know it is for them—everyone in the theater
mirroring the crescent of listeners on screen.
And this is how it is before they buy the store in a few years

and then can't come as often. Later, my grandfather's older brother
will move back to México, where in Torreón he'll host stars
filming in Durango. *Here I am right next to Hollywood,*

Grandfather says, *and he's out golfing with James Garner,*
then throwing a party for Edmond O'Brien
and touring the sets of Westerns.

But I hear *Jane Gardner,* and for years think he meant Ava Gardner,
picture her as she is in *The Night of the Iguana,* under moonlight,
dancing more with the ocean than the two men who accompany her.

Watching it now, the waves laugh at my mistake
as they splash about her hips, the storm drawing near,
and my grandfather's laughter sounds in them too.

FRONT-ROW GIANTS

Rita Hayworth and Glenn Ford are love twenty times our size—their appetite to reach *The End*. They are so many places at once—on theater screens in Los Angeles, New York, Miami, why not Paris—it's as if they've lived a thousand times. She never stops flinging her hair back, never stops the strip tease with her black glove until it's true we know they've *done it*. We can see their world, the light spilling out through the curling smoke. We want to follow their parade of guitar solos, gypsy dances, *have-we-met-before* looks. But just as quickly, they're gone—maybe Ford to the Old West and Hayworth to a backstory in Shanghai. But they meet again in Cordoba, then Trinidad, every time disappearing behind the Columbia Pictures banner.

AMARGOSA OPERA HOUSE

We missed the flowers because there hadn't been enough rain.
We sisters and our parents stand at the salt formations,
the ancient swamp bed now white as bone, gray lines in a cracked plate.

On the drive home, we stop for an eighty-year-old ballerina
who still performs in her toe shoes.

She dances weekly before her painted audience—
the theater's surrounding mural of spectators
from sixteenth-century Spain—their majesties, dukes,
friars, the whole ensemble watching her on tiptoe.

In forty-seven years, she's seen the wildflowers come twice.
She knows what's enough.

estela *[es-TELL-la]* noun (f) :

The anecdote is that my lover's mother,
before he was born, was a coyote
and knew this certain place
in a fence through which to pass—

meaning *the wake from a boat,*
the trail of vapor from a plane,
the slipstream whose current guides.
I read her too in *estrella,* meaning *star.*

CROSSINGS UNACCOMPANIED

✳

This time, there's no swing set in the sandbox
that stretches for miles, no patches
of creosote and saguaro to shade you.
Instead you've swung from the arms of your abuela
into the hills, into the desert, into the river, into the town
of house lights, none of which are yours.

✳

You've almost memorized the phone number
written on a scrap of paper in your pocket
alongside your yellow yo-yo and the red string
between its two hemispheres.
In the other pocket, the prayer card,
except at night, it's too dark to read. Still,
you look up, praying from a list of your own:
Mamá, Papá, tus abuelos, el perro,
your brother somewhere in the stars,
and this may be the one you're following
because sometimes there are rides
to the next town and the next.
Each day the yo-yo unfurls
and springs back to its nest. It sings
faintly in a language of tides.
It flings to the edge of prayer.
It twirls back to your palm in answer. You pray
for your feet to stop aching,
for you to disappear,
a leaf over deep water far downstream.

THE OTHER SIDE OF GIVING

In the town of still shadows, handsewn life-sized dolls
stand where husbands and sons used to be.
The dolls wear their old clothes, their belts, their socks,
but the boots are still walking since wife and daughter put them on
to muck out the chicken coop, to push the barrow of dry earth,
wishing for rain, for water. In the women's dreams,
money is on its way. There will be enough soon, enough.
The women can't say this. Their eyes smudge, as bits of their bodies
fall loose into the wind. They can't say this as they kneel
before the land, its seeds blowing away.

TRAZAR UN MAPA

We learn the city during construction
by glimpsing the familiar down crossroads,
by disappearing under trees. We must
rejoin our road through the belly of a knot.

My love tells me his uncle,
the one who made chairs for a living,
advised: *Cuando te regresas para la casa,*
siempre tienes que regresar por otro lado
en caso de que alguien te busca.

When you return home,
always go another way
in case someone is looking for you.

hablar *[ah-BLAHR]* verb :

The parrot chooses not to speak.
Or say so when tired of teaching it.

Keep a room for only that language.
Place the birdcage inside the room.

Whistle and coo—
find the parrot teaching you.

VALENTINE TO THE DISAPPEARED

Dearest, the hum of a hundred years
finds you in the divided flesh of an orange
tracing you back to northern Chihuahua.

Once-wealthy ancestors are now
a caricature of large heads and long legs. They say,
Even on horses, their feet dragged on the ground.

After the Revolution, you belonged
to fruit-pickers, grocers, motel owners.
Now there's a judge, a professor, less Chihuahua.

Some of us have forgotten how to speak with those dead,
which means, a boy made to feel ashamed in his learning
the language will not learn. He cannot teach his daughters.

Now the feeling returns in me for not knowing the words.
I am told half of you means *bucket* (balde),
and the other means *branch* (rama): water for grafted trees.

I call you *little name* because you turn invisible
in new mouths, have been spoken by so many
you can't be heard anymore.

Little name, as myself, I've always been ready
to send you away like a nutshell boat
weighted down by a pebble into dry streambeds.

It is like that with anything built
to be given.

STUDY OF THE ENCLOSURE

Tiger is pacing from one side to the other—
one side open to hands and speech, the other to echo.
Its ears point forward then back.

A whirlpool of shadows orbits.

Tiger spends its day confused until it sees
a focal point of shivering grass. Crouching, it stalks
a swallow collecting mud and tufts of its fur.

Build a nest from earth, and encase the world before the opening eye.

Darkness nears. We squint toward the tiger, barely visible.
In *The Treasure of the Sierra Madre,* no one knew it was gold
dust and not sand poured out, blown back up to the mountain.

Its yellow eyes may be watching. Could we let them be
abandoned to the wind in kind?

TWO GLASSES

For Great-Grandpa Pedro, God is one of two empty glasses
one night in Inglewood when my father is in law school
and his grandma has been talking about Jesus.

Here we are, positioning them apart on the table, *here's God.*
Then he shrugs his shoulders, tosses his hands in the air.

panza *[PAHN-sah]* noun (f) :

After four children, her shape is lonely
for the time she was most happy.

She practices locating her core in dance—
hula and flamenco at the Senior Center

where, the youngest of the elderly, she feels like a teenager
again. In performances, my sisters and I fold back
into the ocean waves of her fingers, her hips, her shore.

CANCIÓN DE CUNA

—a lullaby for children affected by the 2018 "zero tolerance" policy

Outside, past the ceiling, la luna lunera
shines up and down the long, dark road.
There, the tails of frogs begin to disappear
with the hum—*Sana sana colita de rana.*
And there, the chicks in the cold are saying, *pío, pío, pío.*
There, the branches of wild plums let fall
their small fruits for crickets and a hungry mouse.
And there, somewhere, your mother is singing to you.

Arrurrú and goodnight and prayers
on the rosary of her fingertips.
Nuestra Señora de las Lágrimas / Our Lady of Tears,
may we all grow a little more by daylight,
as does the olive, as does the orchard.

WATER THEORY

*

If the moon's surface was composed of waves
the way da Vinci thought, moon ocean
reflecting the sun and our dark seas' faint glow,

borders might be understood in temperatures, or currents,
or light—fish sustaining themselves in the cold rock,
the warped water, our planet at arm's length like a hot pearl.

*

During red tide, the waves
bring jellyfish you don't see until you do.
A lifeguard washes stings with a spray bottle of vinegar.

On Cornish beaches, reports say Legos
have washed up since 1997 when a shipment was lost.
Occasionally, a sea monster arrives—
a thirteen-foot oarfish, a log covered in goose barnacles.

*

Third graders learn about the universal solvent.
But there are always exceptions:
during the density experiment—in water,
oil and honey divide into colored rings.

In the Great Salt Lake, some tourists in their hats
bob like corks all day, all day in the green water.

*

Monet's bridge over the lily pond
is a dark curve in reflection. In *Impression, Sunrise,*
his bay dashes blue and orange on a wash of faded violet.
Nothing concludes in the current—
through and through—

Have you seen the video of the zebra
attacked by the lion? The lion clamps on the zebra's neck,
but the zebra lowers her further into water.
Out of breath, the lion must let go.

THE RIVER

The river arrives from high heels, crossed legs, pregnancy.
Who knows? It's dappling her thigh now in purple,
green reeds, and yellow mushrooms.

Bog turtle, salamander, pink river dolphin
gathered here in jars, exist in her along shallows
shaded by overgrown trees, the narrow hulls of boats nesting.

Some say my mother's spider veins are drowned water
from the Ice Age, when the original stream was flooded over.
And if that's true, her veins are less a map and more
a pattern of lightning strikes.

Once we were all in the estuary of her.
Once we were axolotl pressing our newfound hands
into the river bottom, pushing off.

NOTES

Spanish definition poems: For immigrants and their descendants, navigating the border between cultures comes with expectations from both sides, often related to language. I address my feelings about being a non-Spanish-speaking Latina in this series in an effort to acknowledge those who do not fit identity categories neatly and who, in turn, help diversify what it means to be Latinx. As an adolescent and adult student of the Spanish language, I lacked an attachment to the words. Here, I teach myself by grafting associative memories to these words, creating a space in which I can belong and grow.

The phonetic renderings were made with the help of Alberto Ríos and *Merriam-Webster's Spanish-English Dictionary* (2003).

"esperanza": The green stripe in the Mexican flag represents independence and hope. The Nahuatl term, "Metztlixcictlico," is the original Aztec word from which the Spanish derived the name México.

"Mexico as Mexico, 1914": This poem takes as its subject the documentary and Hollywood filming of the Mexican Revolution, when Pancho Villa signed a contract with Mutual Film Corporation in 1914 to help fund supplies, and the migration to the U.S. border of those fleeing the violence. *The Life of General Villa*, directed by Christy Cabanne and Raoul Walsh (uncredited), debuted that same year in New York City's Lyric Theater but was taken out of circulation sometime following Villa's 1916 raid in Columbus, New Mexico when U.S. support was withdrawn. The poem also includes imagery from recovered footage of the war filmed by the cinematographer, Charles Rosher, who worked on the 1912 documentary *Life of Villa*. Sources for this research include: *True West*'s "Pancho's Lost Film" by Allen Barra (2016), *LA Times*'s "Pancho Villa, leader of the Mexican Revolution and Hollywood movie star" by Reed Johnson (2010), and the documentary film *Los Rollos Perdidos de Pancho Villa,* directed by Gregorio Rocha (2003).

"Study of Two Hands": One strategy for assessing portraiture is to simultaneously look at the painting and the subject of the painting in a mirror, in order to flatten the subject and better compare the two. Leonardo da Vinci writes about this tactic in Volume I of his notebooks. In the Jean Paul Richter translation, da Vinci asks, "Why are paintings seen more correctly in a mirror than out of it?" and follows with a response in a section entitled "How The Mirror Is The Master [And Guide] Of Painters." This is still used in art classes today.

"Fragmented Apology, 2006": California Senate Bill No. 670, Chapter 663, enacted the "Apology Act for the 1930s Mexican Repatriation Program," which went into effect on January 1, 2006, in response to the forced deportation of two million people of Mexican ancestry in the 1930s, including roughly 400,000 American citizens. Many are unaware of this. The *Los Angeles Daily News* reported: "California's apology was inspired by the work of...Francisco Balderrama and Raymond Rodrïguez." Their book is entitled *Decade of Betrayal* (University of New Mexico Press, 1995).

"To Reach the Middle of the Ocean," "Santa Catalina," "USS *Randolph* **Damaged, 1945," and "Ulithi":** These poems were written with the aid of interviews with my paternal grandfather, Enrique Balderrama, who served in the Merchant Marines in WWII. While these civilian mariners operated in war zones and suffered many casualties, they were not granted active-duty status and were therefore not eligible for VA benefits until 1988.

Other sources for these poems include: *BBC Future*'s "The quest to save the Hollywood bison" by Jason G. Goldman (2014), *KCET*'s "Lost LA" article: "Commandos and Anti-Aircraft Guns: Catalina's Top-Secret WWII History" by Nathan Masters (2013), Encyclopedia Britannica's "Ulithi Atoll" (updated 2013), *Naval History and Heritage*

Command's Dictionary of American Fighting Ships: "USS *Randolph* (CV 15)" (updated 2009), *The Forgotten Heroes: The Heroic Story of the United States Merchant Marine* by Brian Herbert (Tom Doherty Associates, 2004), a documentary episode from *The Sea Hunters*: "Human Torpedoes: The Wreck of the USS *Mississinewa*" (aired 2003), and *LA Times*'s "After 40 Years, Merchant Marines Win Veteran Status: Finally—a 'Flag and a Headstone'" by Eric Lichtblau (1988).

"Ulithi": Ulithi is a volcanic atoll comprised of roughly forty islets in the Caroline Islands in the Pacific and served as a major staging area for the U.S. Navy at the end of WWII. At the height of operation, Ulithi's lagoon stretching between fifteen and twenty-two miles across was an anchorage for 700 ships. Sunken warships, including the USS *Mississinewa*, still rest there.

"Water, 2014": Facts are drawn from these 2014 articles: *CNN*'s "More children crossing U.S.-Mexico border alone" by Nick Valencia, *New York Times*'s "Children at the Border" by Haeyoun Park, *NPR*'s "Amid Wave of Child Immigrants, Reports of Abuse by Border Patrol" by John Burnett, and *Think Progress*'s "What It's Really Like To Cross The U.S.-Mexico Border" by Jack Jenkins. The poem also includes details from Guillermo Galindo's 2016 visual art presentation entitled "Sonic Border," part of the Utah Museum of Fine Art's "ARTlandish" series. In this multi-sensory performance, Galindo presented and played instruments he handcrafted from objects found near the U.S.-Mexico border.

"Zero, 2018": The U.S. "zero tolerance" policy was enforced April 2018 on illegal immigrants, which included a separation of families, resulting in 2000+ immigrant children being separated from their parents or guardians over six weeks. Additionally, the empty shell is believed to be the Mayan representation for zero.

"Alternate Ways to Paint": I believe we carry a personal history in us, an archaeology of attachment we often can't help but project on other surfaces. In this loose ekphrasis, I've glanced off Picasso's artworks and drawn associations to my family mythology. Titles are those of Picasso's paintings and drawings, translated from the French—which the Spanish artist most often used—with slight variations.

The series is also a PetchaKucha—a form derived from Japanese business presentations in which there are twenty slides, for which the presenter speaks twenty seconds on each. I was introduced to this form during workshops at the City University of Hong Kong while attending a Virginia G. Piper Center Creative Writing Fellowship.

"In Bed with the Lion": This poem is an ekphrasis of a photo in a series by Michael Rougier for *LIFE* magazine. Taken in 1971, the photos depict Tippi Hedren and her teenaged daughter, Melanie Griffith, sharing their mansion with a lion in preparation for the film *Roar*. The images are now at the Getty.

"Lion Lights": Richard Turere, at the age of thirteen, gave a 2013 TED Talk with this title on his invention to protect livestock near the Kenyan savanna.

"Witness": This poem includes information from *Nature*'s "Significant plastic accumulation on the Cocos (Keeling) Islands, Australia" by J.L. Lavers et al. (2019) and language quoted in *The Guardian*'s "Francis and Sophie's secret: girl who hugged pope delivers immigration plea" by Lauren Gambino (2015).

"Some Horses": From fall 2015 to spring 2016, I volunteered for the Arizona State's Prison Education Program by co-teaching a creative writing workshop at the Arizona Department of Corrections State

Prison in Florence, Arizona. Corrals across the street from the prison are visible upon entry. Their Wild Horse Program through Arizona Correctional Industries and the Bureau of Land Management allows inmates to domesticate mustangs under the guidance of experienced trainers, so that the horses can be offered for adoption.

"Spanish Language Film House, 1930s": Spanish song lyrics are from *Cuesta abajo*, a 1934 film directed by Louis J. Gasnier, and the tango by the same name written by Alfredo Le Pera.

"Amargosa Opera House": The Amargosa Opera House and Hotel, located in Death Valley Junction, California, was in a state of disrepair until Marta Becket began transforming it in 1968. According to their official website, she pursued a vision to "celebrate art in the desert" and performed until 2012. She passed away in 2017 at the age of 92, but her legacy continues in weekend performances October-May.

"Water Theory": I was inspired while visiting Leonardo da Vinci's "Codex Leicester" temporarily on display at the Phoenix Art Museum in 2015. On one page, da Vinci hypothesizes that the moon has an ocean. Throughout its phases, the light part is the moon's ocean reflected, and the subtle glow in the dark part is the result of sunlight reflecting Earth's oceans onto the moon's. The moon is spotted and uneven because of "wind-driven waves."

"The River": The details from this poem were derived from the history of the Hudson River during my stay at the Ashbery Homeschool in the summer of 2014.

ACKNOWLEDGMENTS

Grateful acknowledgment is made to the editors of the following journals in which these poems, or versions of these poems, appeared:

Anomaly (*Drunken Boat*): "The Other Side of Giving"
Blackbird: "Accountability for Blind Sheep," "Canción de Cuna," and "Zero, 2018"
Cider Press Review: "In Bed with the Lion"
The Citron Review: "Lion Lights"
Connotation Press: "Valentine to the Disappeared," "Water, 2014," and "The Dead Dream Us"
Existere: "Fragmented Apology, 2006" and "Afterlife"
Halophyte Zine: "Trazar un Mapa"
Interim: "oscuro," "rueda," and "huerta"
Miramar: "The Queen of Technicolor, 1943"
The Missing Slate: "A Fire to Cook"
New Ohio Review: "Now in Color"
New Plains Review: "The River"
Poet Lore: "You and I Saw Animals"
Public Pool: "esperanza," "salvaje," and "Some Horses"
Qu Literary Magazine: "Water Theory"
San Pedro River Review: "Ulithi"
Southern Humanities Review: "Finger Puppet in the Likeness of Frida Kahlo"
Spillway: "Amargosa Opera House"

This book was made possible by the contributions of love and support from so many and especially due to the hard work of my parents, grandparents, and earlier ancestors, who first called this country home and aspired to create a better life for their children.

I am indebted to the generous support of my committee and community at Arizona State University. Thank you to Alberto Ríos, Sally Ball, and Cynthia Hogue as well as Beckian Fitzgoldberg, Norman Dubie, T.R. Hummer, and my MFA cohort. Your guidance and friendship deeply aided the first drafts of these poems.

Muchas gracías to Francisco Aaragon and the Letras Latinas literary initiative at the University of Notre Dame. Being welcomed into this community was so important for the advancement of this project. I'd like to extend personal thanks to the 2013 cohort with whom I first participated—Lauren Espinoza, Melisa Garcia, Ae Hee Lee, Kelsey Castenada, and Steve Castro—for your vulnerability, friendship, and inclusion.

Thank you to the Virginia G. Piper Center for Creative Writing. Your Writing Residency Fellowship and Creative Writing Fellowship permitted me the chance to write in diverse and enriching spaces. Experiences during these travels continue to influence my work. Also much gratitude to my fellow travelers—Angie Dell, Gary Garrison, Naomi Telushkin, Lauren Albin, Elissa Hutson, Sue Hyon Bae, Aria Curtis, and Melissa Pritchard. I will hold those memories in my heart always.

Thank you to the University of Utah, which awarded me the Mabey Poetry Prize to help fund the submission of this manuscript to presses and contests. I am grateful for the feedback from Katharine Coles, Paisley Rekdal, and Jacqueline Osherow and her workshop, who read and offered feedback to full manuscripts, with special recognition to friends: Liza Flum, Ceridwen Hall, and Paula Mendoza on many of these poems.

Thank you, Sandra Ang, Michelle Macfarlane, and Emily Dyer Barker, for your love and hospitality during the summer of 2018. I enjoyed our meetings and motivating conversations that nurtured each of our personal goals, among them this book.

Thank you to the University of California, Riverside, where my studies in creative writing first began. Christopher Buckley, thank you for inviting me to your graduate workshop at UCR and for introducing me to the possibility of continuing my studies in creative writing. Thank you, Juan Felipe Herrera, for your mentorship and zeal for life and poems. Your freshman class was a true joy where friends, Veronica Alley and Grace Kang, were my first writing community.

Thank you also to my UCR professors in fiction: Susan Straight, Michael Jayme, Charmaine Craig, Andrew Winer, and Goldberry Long. Your lessons on how to tell good stories have stayed with me.

Kitt Keller and Lauren Albin, thank you for going above and beyond with your generous feedback. I hope we can continue exchanging work in the future.

Jenny Molberg, thank you for seeing the potential in this project and for your great advice to push the poems just a bit further.

Thank you to all my teachers who have instilled in me a love of writing. Mrs. Smith, thank you for your poetry section in high school. Mr. Murguia, I think of your AP Literature class often.

Thank you to all my Spanish teachers throughout the years, including Mrs. Bruton, Mr. Martinez, Danielle Riggs, and my husband, Chuy. However slowly, it's a journey I continue pursuing.

Thank you to Perugia Press, especially Rebecca Hart Olander, for selecting this project and working closely with me through the editorial and publication process. I'm honored to become part of Perugia's writer community.

Lastly, I am deeply appreciative for all the love and encouragement I've received over the years from my family. I am especially grateful for my paternal grandparents, Enrique (Hank) and Celia (Sally). Thank you for lending me your stories and instilling the value of education in your family. Thank you to my Aunt Vicky for reading and celebrating my writing in high school when I was interested in fantasy; to my godfather, Uncle Frank, for your kind correspondence during my studies; to my parents, Ann and Lorenzo, for your unyielding support and enthusiasm; and to my dear sisters—Elizabeth, Katherine, and Mary—for making the life we share so much sweeter. Thank you always to my husband, Chuy, for your love, listening ear, and all our long drives together. And to my little bird, Georgia, for your company when it was just us and poems in a small, quiet room.

ABOUT THE AUTHOR

Jacqueline Balderrama lives and teaches in Salt Lake City, where she is a doctoral candidate in literature and creative writing at the University of Utah. She is the author of the chapbook *Nectar and Small* (Finishing Line Press, 2019) and a poetry editor for *Iron City Magazine* and *Quarterly West*. Balderrama has been involved in the Letras Latinas literary initiative, the ASU Prison Education Program, and the Wasatch Writers in the Schools.

ABOUT PERUGIA PRESS

Perugia Press publishes one collection of poetry each year, by a woman at the beginning of her publishing career. Our mission is to produce beautiful books that interest longtime readers of poetry and welcome those new to poetry. We also aim to celebrate and promote poetry whenever we can, and to keep the cultural discussion of poetry inclusive.

Also from Perugia Press:

* *Hail and Farewell,* Abby E. Murray
* *Girldom,* Megan Peak
* *Starshine Road,* L. I. Henley
* *Brilliance, Spilling: Twenty Years of Perugia Press Poetry*
* *Guide to the Exhibit,* Lisa Allen Ortiz
* *Grayling,* Jenifer Browne Lawrence
* *Sweet Husk,* Corrie Williamson
* *Begin Empty-Handed,* Gail Martin
* *The Wishing Tomb,* Amanda Auchter
* *Gloss,* Ida Stewart
* *Each Crumbling House,* Melody S. Gee
* *How to Live on Bread and Music,* Jennifer K. Sweeney
* *Two Minutes of Light,* Nancy K. Pearson
* *Beg No Pardon,* Lynne Thompson
* *Lamb,* Frannie Lindsay
* *The Disappearing Letters,* Carol Edelstein
* *Kettle Bottom,* Diane Gilliam
* *Seamless,* Linda Tomol Pennisi
* *Red,* Melanie Braverman
* *A Wound On Stone,* Faye George
* *The Work of Hands,* Catherine Anderson
* *Reach,* Janet E. Aalfs
* *Impulse to Fly,* Almitra David
* *Finding the Bear,* Gail Thomas

The text of this book is set in ITC Legacy Serif, a 1993 revival of Nicolas Jensen's classic fifteenth-century typeface designs by Ronald Arnholm, which combines a legible design adapted for contemporary printing methods with centuries-old classic letterforms. The companion italic faces follow the sixteenth-century design patterns of Claude Garamond. Poem titles and other display type are set in Basic Sans, a 2016 family from Latinotype by Daniel Hernández. The grotesque-style sans serif is clean and simple, yet offers subtle, idiosyncratic details in its letterforms. The title typeface, Phosphate Inline, is a 2010 digital revival by Steve Jackaman and Ashley Muir of Phosphor, a 1930 display face designed by Jakob Erbar for the German founder Ludwig and Meyer and so named because the inline design creates a convincing optical illusion of glowing.